Pen to Paper

Chloe Miles

BookLeaf Publishing

Presentation by *BookLeaf Publishing*

Web: www.bookleafpub.com

E-mail: info@bookleafpub.com

ISBN: 9789357210461

First edition 2022

DEDICATION

For the friends who believed in my ability to create, and encouraged me to step out of my comfort zone.

The Shadow at the Door

Once upon a different time,
As tales of caution show,
Sat strange a dwelling on the moor,
Where none would ever go,

It once had been a happy place,
In years that came before,
But happiness departed with
One tap upon the door,

The laughter fled, all joy escaped,
And darkness dwelt alone,
A haunting spectre in the chair,
A king upon a throne,

Which first rose in the twilight,
As it crept across the moor,
And visited that lonely house,
The shadow at the door,

As stonework crumbled, weeds grew up,
And wood began to rot,
And soon that place became the house
That all but one forgot,

For burnished in their memory,

The dark rooms on the moor,
And horror that accompanied
The shadow at the door,

And all the while, living beyond
The threshold none dared cross,
The spectre fed off memories
Of tragedy and loss,

The darkness still sits waiting
For the gate to creak once more,
But nobody would dare to greet
The shadow at the door.

The Morning Chorus

As daylight breaks between the trees,
While sunbeams warm the earth with ease,
There comes upon the gentle breeze
the tweets to say hello,

They wake the world from slumbers deep,
With many high and cheerful cheep,
To bring the weary from their sleep,
To waking world they go,

And though there's some who might complain,
About symphonious refrain,
When Winter comes to earth again,
How quickly they would know,

If trees weren't filled with nature's song,
As single voices join the throng,
Within a trice they soon would long
For music down below,

Between the notes that glide and trill,
Lie melodies that soar and thrill,
Which warm cold hearts, remove the chill,
With chirpy, cheery tune,

So celebrate the birds who sing,
The joyful music of the Spring,
And optimism that they bring,
After the Winter gloom.

Hidden

Do you ever stop to wonder what's hidden
behind the mask?
Underneath the feigned politeness
that weaves words of sincerity,
so convincing to others,
that to suggest a lack of true feeling
would seem wholly disingenuous.

The charming smile,
which does not quite form creases
that nestle in the corners of the eyes,
Rendering a face
that should be suffused with warmth on its
production,
to a replica of happiness;

An alabaster statue, a model ready for carving,
Lifelike, but no more real than the echo of
laughter
that sits hollow and flat,
Unable to bridge the gulf,
mend the cracks,
fill the silence beneath.

For behind the mask that fools the world,

keeping away the concerned frowns
that would grow to unwelcome intervention,
lies a pervading, consuming melancholy,
Which, if revealed for what it is,
would not be quite so pleasing to the beholder.

So the mask stays firmly in place,
And the world remains none the wiser.

You'll Find Me

Don't cry for me, as I drift deep
far from the realms of dreams and sleep,
Though where I am, you cannot go,
above the clouds, sun, rain and snow,

Don't fill your heart with tears and sorrow,
I could not stay to see tomorrow,
Or lift your head to curse the skies
in voice that's lost in strangled cries,

I won't be found in flesh and bone,
that mortal house no more my home,
As repose beckons beyond life,
away from pain and daily strife,

You'll find me in the playful breeze
that floats the autumn leaves off trees,
And causes them to dance in glee,
to celebrate their being free,

Or in the late sun's gentle glow,
before it dips and sinks below,
The light it casts like pooling gold,
that banishes all thoughts of cold,

I'm found within the robin's song,
continuing as nights grow long,
Sweet melodies that fill the air,
notes drifting through without a care,

I'm there between the lapping waves
that spray soft sand with salty haze,
And shelter life within the deep,
whose secrets I will safely keep,

You'll recognise me in the sky,
I'm twinkling down from stars on high,
And safely guide the lost back home,
to places where they're loved and known,

So do not weep and do not mourn,
you'll find me here from dusk to dawn,
I'll be always, as memories fade,
within your heart 'til end of days.

Solipsism

Imagine if all of life was a lie
told by the Gods who reign on high,
and really we were never here,
and they could make us disappear,

Imagine if the things we're taught,
originality of thought
and free will, were just falsehoods told
to convince us that we're not controlled,

If all the choices that we made
were just part of the games they played,
Our loves and losses, hopes and dreams
just entertainment on their screens,

How could the truth ever be known
if all our thoughts were not our own?
All of our actions preordained,
like circus monkeys, carefully trained,

How convenient it would be to blame
our actions on some Godly game,
Determinism to help us flee
our moral responsibility.

But, what is true? We'll never know,
much safer then to act as though
our thoughts and feelings can affect
the choices that we will make next...

Breaking News

I came across a dragon egg,
The shell was very large,
I thought it probably should be warm,
So kept it in the bath,

I wondered where its mother was,
And if she'd ever know,
Where she could find her precious egg,
While it continued to grow,

The shell expanded day-by-day,
A marbled blue and green,
I thought it was the prettiest egg
That I had ever seen,

One day I came into the room,
And noticed something strange,
The colour on the marbled shell,
Was undergoing change,

A swirling red and burning orange
Slowly started to show,
Then through the colours of the sea
Spread a gentle, fiery glow,

While criss-crossed on the surface
Was the faintest little crack,
Which started on the front and worked
Its way around the back,

I knew the egg was going to hatch,
My apprehension grew,
For who knew how much damage
Day-old dragons could still do?

Then finally with a little crunch,
A snout popped out the top,
Two beady eyes fixed on my face,
Time almost seemed to stop,

It stretched its small mouth open wide,
The shower head was ready,
To deal with any sudden blaze,
My aim was true and steady,

It let out an almighty yawn,
And curled into a ball,
Then softly snored as it slept on,
Not really a threat at all,

I tucked it carefully up in bed,
Ever the obliging host,
And in the morning, when it woke,
I made it beans on toast,

It wolfed its brunch down happily,
Then wandered straight outside,
Looking longingly upwards at the sky,
It stretched its wings out wide,

It beat its small wings once or twice,
And hovered off the ground,
Then flew off in the distance,
with one final glance around.

Circumvention

All the world before you, and yet still
so easy to fall into that trap
of middle-class presumption,
and the inevitable checklist
of moments that must be ticked off
as the years pass.

Your path in life laid out before you,
like a carefully charted map.
Societal expectations hanging over you,
like a guillotine, ready to make its final
descent.
Beheading those deviating ambitions
that have wandered off
the familiar path.

While all around, voices clamour
like a host of chattering magpies.
How convenient they should be called
a parliament,
mischief,
or murder.

The Fairy Ball

Deep within a leafy grove,
There is a place where wild things rove,
Both light of foot and heavy paw,
From tiny squeak to fearsome roar,

The place where lonely creatures come,
To hear the beating of the drum,
They leave behind their fears and woes,
To meet as friends and not as foes,

A gentle fluting fills the air,
Played by the fairies dwelling there,
From silver pipes it is released,
The music that can tame a beast,

They come here both the great and small,
Each creature living in the thrall,
And with no thought, no care at all,
They join in with the Fairy Ball,

The creatures dance and moonbeams shine,
They lose all sense of passing time,
As hours and minutes seem to slow,
Beneath the glittering night sky's glow,

Of food and drink they have no need,
Too lost within the dance to feed,
Claws, paws and feet all stamp as one,
They move until the rising sun,

Then one by one, they drift away,
All sloping off to face the day,
Until no trace is left at all,
Of twilight's latest Fairy Ball.

Silence

Silence slowly creeping in
while conversations lull and dim,
until the breaking wave of thought
spills slowly down, no fight is fought.

Where words abounded, full of dreams,
transformed from oceans to mere streams,
the inkwell is no longer tapped,
the flow dries up, the pen is capped.

The pauses grow, their tone conveys
a meaning more than shifted gaze,
the loudest sound is hearts that beat
in dissonant time, the split complete.

The storm will never manifest,
cacophony of noise depressed,
it falls to earth like trickling rain,
words never to be heard again.

If There Was Such a Thing as Unicorns

If there was such a thing as unicorns,
I have not one shred of doubt
that before too long the bounty would
leave someone's bank account,

And the poachers wouldn't care how rare,
they'd see the unicorn
as a sham medicinal product,
grinding powder from its horn,

If there was such a thing as unicorns
it soon would be confined,
and the videos of it circling
in messages and online,

And the masses would all visit it
if cooped up in the zoo,
until something else distracted them
within a week or two,

If there was such a thing as unicorns
we'd see it on the news
as a novelty, a funny meme,
not a life form we abuse,

And it wouldn't be too long before
they all would go extinct,
just another unfortunate species
we'd have driven to the brink,

So I'm glad there are no unicorns
for us to traumatise,
they would bring out the worst bits of us
that we all try to disguise.

Fire and Ice

Burning fury, searing pain,
Thoughts that tumble, wax and wane,
Piercing cold like ice in waves,
Numbness that the body craves,

Navigates a fog of thought,
Loss of time, all come to naught,
Rage, inferno blazing high,
Snuffed out with an icy sigh,

Questions unanswered dance around,
They tease and taunt but make no sound,
A need to scream to find release,
To lay to rest, and come to peace,

Dreams unfulfilled are swept away,
Cobwebs unfit to see the day,
Memories and moments with meaning lost,
Glacial heart with each day's frost,

Fire and ice conflict, compete,
Neither ready for defeat,
While fire still smoulders, ice settles in,
Ready for winter to begin.

Instant-likes

Fix up the smile and chisel the jaw,
Nipping that waist in a little bit more,

Slim down those calves and enlarge the chest,
Upload and wait to see who loves me best,

Witty one-liner to serve as a caption,
Borrowed from someone with minor adaption,

Use it to judge whether people adore me,
Going by love hearts attached to the story,

After all, who cares what's real and what's not?
When self-worth is how many likes that you got.

Broken People

Can you even really remember the last time that you felt whole,
As if something wasn't missing from the core of your very soul,

Fragmented, like a puzzle with an absent corner piece
which, with one minor misplacement, will now never be complete,

While books promising transformation and improvement fill our shelves,
Other people seek fulfilment through their 'perfect' online selves,

There are some who'll use sex, drugs or money to try and fill the gap,
While others go more wholesome, having children or a cat,

But at the end of the day, we're all simply trying to fill the gaping void,
To remove the empty feeling that we all want to avoid,

So maybe we're all broken and we feel it deep inside,
But maybe being broken is just part of being alive.

Vacuum

Nocturnal noises lost within
mankind's infernal, wretched din,
Shouts, hoots and whistles echo round,
the fragile peace no longer found.

A heavy sky sits dull at night
with just the merest hint of light,
the tender glow of luminous stars
snuffed out by street lamps, signs and cars.

But far above where humans play,
no sentient Gods to whom they pray,
Just blackness stretching ever high
beyond their concept of the sky.

For deep within the cosmic bliss
exists a vast, unknown abyss,
where human chaos cannot reach
and deafening preachers cannot preach.

Walking Away

There was no prior warning before she
disappeared.
No impeccably crafted note to justify the
absence.
Indeed, nobody to notice that the kettle wasn't
switched on at 6am
with a satisfying click,
followed by the pop of the toaster
and general hustle and bustle of a morning
routine,
perfected and honed by one alone
in a two up, two down house
that she did not own.

In fact, the first acknowledgement of the
disappearance
was the Monday morning,
when the missing-ness was first felt by someone,
frustrated by the burden of extra work,
confused by the lack of communication.

No response at home resulted in
concerned calls to next of kin.
Nobody had heard.
The visit to the house showed

everything she owned left behind.

Everything except:
one pair of trainers, rucksack, purse.
As if she had just walked away from her life,
never to look back.

Stage Fright

Gavin was simply an ordinary boy,
for whom speaking publicly didn't bring joy,

In fact it brought terror, simple and plain,
he never ever ever wanted to do it again,

Sadly, his class teacher didn't agree,
she didn't get how scary speaking could be,

So every day she would choose someone new,
to talk about themselves for a minute or two,

And yesterday came fateful words that brought sorrow,
"Don't forget Gavin, it's your turn tomorrow,"

The last time he'd tried hadn't gone well at all,
he'd run out the classroom and started to bawl,

The class were left howling, their laughter so loud,
and that was the last time, or so he had vowed.

Gavin was nervous, Gavin was scared,

Gavin felt awfully underprepared,

His knees knocked together, his arms and legs shook,
his heart banged with every step that he took,

He opened his mouth and attempted to speak,
but all that came out was a singular squeak.

His eyes filled with tears, his cheeks burned with shame,
he waited for laughter, but none of it came.

Instead from the front row his friends held up signs,
that read 'Go Gavin!' and 'You've got it this time!'

He took a deep breath, firmly planted his feet,
then he opened his mouth and started to speak.

A Very British Welcome

"Keep out the refugees!" they say,
"Don't let the masses in!
It's their fault that they left their land,
why should we welcome them?"

No matter that they're tossed on waves
or that they're forced to flee,
while others lounge in comfort
sipping smugly on their tea,

As boats sink in the ocean
crammed with countless, desperate souls,
to stop them ever coming
still remains the primary goal,

Yes, they've got their mobiles with them,
can you really begrudge phones,
when for most it is the lifeline
that connects them to their homes?

Could you leave your possessions, loved ones,
and your job behind,
when the life that you were hoping for
is not the one you find?

And yet, if it were us,
we really wouldn't understand
why others didn't welcome us

and lend a helping hand,

If our people were the ones in need,
were scared and full of fear,
we'd expect these countries to step up
and keep the entrance clear,

Somehow we seem to forget
that they are human beings too,
that in another life and time
these people could be me or you,

Meanwhile, upon a boat that tips
and sways from side to side,
there are people fleeing war and terror,
genocide and knives,

While all we seem to care about
is our own festive cheer,
spending millions on fireworks
to welcome in the year,

So instead of wasting money
that goes up in flames and smoke,
we could consider helping those
who need a bit of hope.

Uncertainties

A hasty step that cracks the ice
awakens those within the depths,
whose sneers and whispers echo round
the chamber where they once had slept.

And creeping upwards they begin
incessant taunts to hurt and shame,
then steal into the mortal world,
creating anguish, fear and pain.

With stealth they slip between the words
of warmth and trust; they suffocate,
extinguishing the guttering light
for shadows then to dominate.

They plant seeds of incertitude,
which root and strangle wisps of truth ,
until full-grown they only bear
a crop of tainted, bitter fruit.

Old Haunts

The ache of memory is unexpected
when you revisit the town where love once
dwelled,
before it dwindled into vapours like the wisp of
cloud that hangs in the blue sky, above the town
you once called
Home.

Where that old familiar road winds down
towards the river,
Where you once laughed deep and long, bedded
down on the picnic rug
that never quite kept out the damp from the
dewy grass.

The floral displays,
a jewel in the crown of the castle,
at which you could once gaze through sashed
windows from the sofa,
Feet nestled into the crook of your legs and a
steaming cup of tea in hand.

The bowling green lined with worn wooden
benches,
Where you sat side-by-side,

Cool drink in hand while you contentedly
surveyed the scene in the summer sun,
or delved into a book while the world carried on
around you.

Each step opens the bank of memories
which had been carefully put away,
Until every bar, cafe, restaurant, shop,
is tagged by a steady stream of
Remember when's.

It's hard to know if it's more painful or cathartic,
Being taken back to a time where both happiness
and misery dwelt,
The place where love was somehow
irretrievably lost,
But it still felt like home all the same.

Winter's Walk

I once was walking in the woods
one frozen winter's day,
when I came across a strange old man
in a state of disarray,

He was pacing round a leafless glade,
his brow was deeply furrowed,
while he stomped across the hardened mud
where slumbering creatures burrowed,

He saw me coming closer
and his frown grew ever deep,
as he threw himself within my path
with one enormous leap,

"Was it you?" he asked in a furious voice
as he wagged his finger my way,
"Was it you??" he demanded again of me;
I wasn't quite sure what to say,

"Was what me?" I cried, bewildered,
as his questions lacked coherence,
awaiting his reply,
I studied closer his appearance,

His face was creased with lines of time
that spoke of many years,
his nose was blue and on his chin
the frost clung to his beard,

His azure eyes shone brightly
like a cloudless winter's sky,
his mouth was firmly set
as he constructed his reply,

Upon his back he seemed to wear
a cloak made out of moss,
while his legs were clothed with dried out
leaves,
his feet in wooden clogs,

I wondered to myself
who this curious man could be,
as he gave a sigh and leaned against
the trunk of a neighbouring tree,

"They all left far too early,
they came out of hibernation,
the temperature, a bit too high,
gave out wrong information,

And now because it's early
they will find that Spring's not ready,
the temperature has dipped again,
the food supply's unsteady,

The birds too aren't migrating
in their usual timely way,
as the balmy summer evenings
caused some of them to delay,

Across the sea the melting ice
is making oceans rise
losing polar bears their homes
and causing storms to fill the skies,

And while you might prefer to have
a summer filled with sun,
the fire and drought it brings
cause only harm to everyone,

Don't even get me started
on the loss of food supplies,
as the carefully planted crops
all shrivel up before our eyes,

And with every year that passes
things are only getting worse,
before too long it'll be too late
to put things in reverse."

With this the old man wept
as he leant against the tree,
and I, confused, asked cautiously,
"But Sir, was what me?"

The old man stopped his weeping,
wiped a hand across his face,
and cast a resigned eye
around the leafless, empty place.

"Was it you," he asked more wearily,
"Who brought about this change?
Are you part of the reason
that the numbers rearrange?

Have you burnt fossil fuels,
so CO2 fills up the air?
Have you cut down and burnt trees,
so the forest isn't there?

Have the cows reared for your burgers
released too much methane,
while the sky fills with emissions
from your frequent flights on planes?

Did you drive instead of walk?
Throw away and not recycle?
Have you ever even thought about
your role within this cycle?"

As I heard his accusations,
I grew more and more ashamed,
then he laid a hand upon my arm,
"There is still time to change."

"But how?" I asked him hopelessly,
"What can one person do?"
He looked at me appraisingly,
"Well, there's some things you could review,

Walk instead of drive,
even better do not fly,
use solar energy for power
from the light that's in the sky,

Eat less meat and dairy,
buy from shops that are nearby,
and next time you're on a shopping spree,
just pause and consider why."

I nodded my head pensively
as I thought what he said through,
for these were things I knew
with some small effort I could do.

At this the old man turned from me
and began to walk away,

"Wait," I called, "Who are you?
Why did you come to the woods today?"

"Winter's the name," he answered
as he strode into the distance,
"I came to start you off
as you maintain the Earth's existence."

I stood there open mouthed
where he left me in the glade,
while with a sort of shimmer,
in the distance, he seemed to fade.

Lullaby for the Troubled Mind

Hush now, my child, you're quite safe here,
there's no need for your dread and fear,
The bombs won't fall on us tonight,
the marching boots are not our plight,

No haunting sirens fill the air,
and swamp our hearts with pure despair,
The sky won't fall around your head,
you're tucked up nice and snug in bed,

Don't cry, my love, you won't miss out
on education, have no doubt,
The starving eyes will not be yours,
as poverty grows and hunger gnaws,

You'll get your three square meals today,
and liberty to run and play,
You won't be huddled underground,
with screams and gunfire all around,

Rest easy, sweet, your life goes on,
your joy and freedom not foregone,
The war you see is far from us,
not our home blasted into dust.

Don't dream of those who cannot sleep,
with trembling ground beneath their feet,
As those they love are massacred,
defiant voice no longer heard,

You will not have to question why,
the roaring flames engulf the sky,
So dream of hope and peace, my dove,
and send Ukraine our thoughts and love.

www.ingramcontent.com/pod-product-compliance
Lightning Source LLC
Chambersburg PA
CBHW051745130826
49812CB00033B/1004
* 9 7 8 9 3 5 7 2 1 0 4 6 1 *